BONE CANCER

Current and Emerging Trends in Detection and Treatment

HEATHER HASAN

ROSEN
PUBLISHING®
New York

To my father-in-law, Dr. Mohammed Hasan, with love

Published in 2009 by The Rosen Publishing Group, Inc.
29 East 21st Street, New York, NY 10010

Library of Congress Cataloging-in-Publication Data

Hasan, Heather.
Bone cancer: current and emerging trends in detection and treatment / Heather Hasan.—1st ed.
     p. cm.—(Cancer and modern science)
Includes bibliographical references and index.
ISBN-13: 978-1-4358-5010-1 (library binding)
1. Bones—Cancer—Popular works. I. Title.
RC280.B6H375 2009
616.99'471—dc22

                                                                                2008019931

Manufactured in the United States of America

On the cover: Colored scanning electron micrograph of bone cancer precursor cells on the surface of a bone

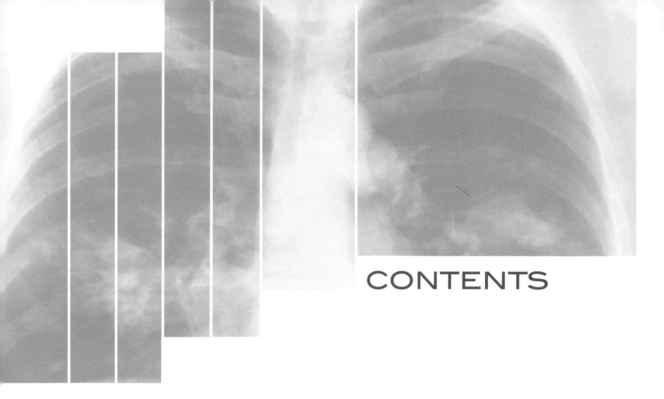

CONTENTS

INTRODUCTION

About 2,500 bone cancer cases are diagnosed in the United States each year. These mainly affect children and adolescents. In 2002, a ten-year-old girl named Erin Sweeney became one of the children whose lives have been changed by the disease. It all started when Erin's mother noticed a small lump on her daughter's right leg. Her parents assumed that she had simply fallen at school, so they were not worried. However, within two weeks, the lump had grown, Erin's leg was swollen, and she was in pain.

Her parents took her to their family doctor for a series of tests. After the doctors reviewed the tests, the Sweeneys were told that their daughter had osteosarcoma. Osteosarcoma is a kind of bone cancer that mainly affects young people. Her cancer was on her femur bone, which is the upper leg bone. When Erin Sweeney heard the word "cancer," she was understandably scared. However, she had much less reason to fear than someone who was in her position years ago.

Cancer has afflicted humans throughout history. Ancient physicians considered cancer patients to be incurable. This view largely persisted,

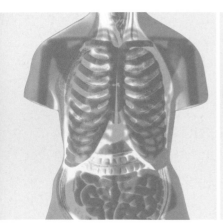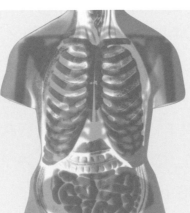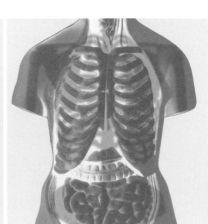

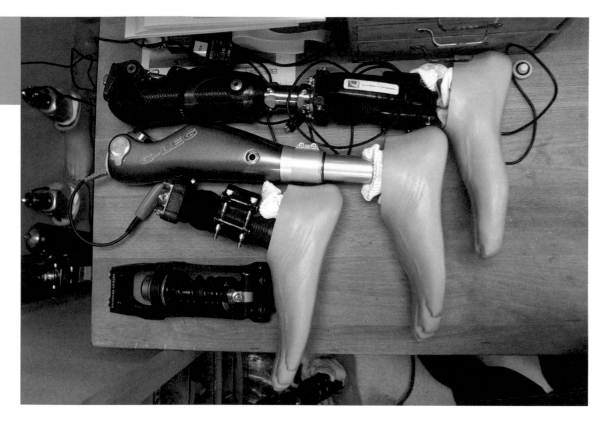

Modern science and technology have led to very advanced replacement limbs (prostheses). These allow those who have lost limbs, such as bone cancer victims, to live more normal lives.

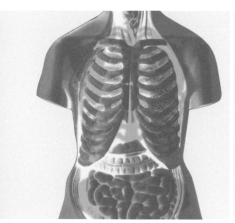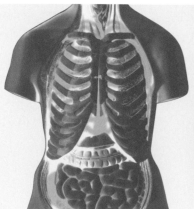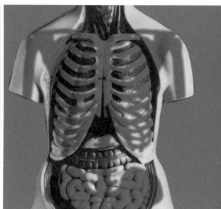

even into the twentieth century, making cancer one of the most feared diseases. However, people with bone cancer are surviving better today than they did even a few years ago. Now, doctors have a much clearer understanding of cancer. They understand what causes it and who might be at risk. In the past, doctors sometimes misdiagnosed bone cancer. By the time they realized it was bone cancer, it was often too late. They did not have the kind of diagnostic tools that we have today. Fortunately, many remarkable advances have been made in this area. New technology makes it possible to diagnose cancer earlier and with more accuracy.

Erin Sweeney is fortunate that she lives at a time when bone cancer treatment is advancing rapidly. Even twenty years ago, the only treatment option for bone cancer patients was amputation, or the removal of the affected limb. Today, most people with bone cancer are treated without removal of the limb. This was the case for Erin. Her infected bone was replaced with a device called Repiphysis. This device contained a specially designed spring that allowed doctors to lengthen it. Thus, the device "grew" as Erin did. She also benefited from other advances in treatment that were unavailable in the past, like radiation treatment and chemotherapy. (These will be discussed later in the book.) No one is more grateful for these kinds of advances than Erin Sweeney and her family. "She's doing really well," said her mother, Terri, a year after her daughter was diagnosed. "She's back to being a normal kid."

In the last ten years, researchers have learned more about bone cancer than in all the centuries that came before. This book serves to educate people about bone cancers such as the one that affected Erin Sweeney. In the following chapters, the types of bone cancer and their risk factors, diagnosis, and treatment will be discussed.

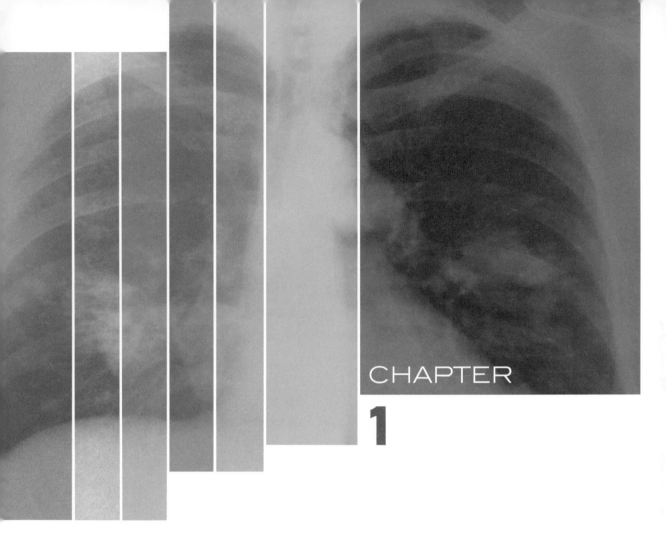

CHAPTER

1

WHAT IS BONE CANCER?

The human body is made up of billions of cells. Cells are the smallest units of all living things. They are so small that they can only be seen with a microscope. Under a microscope, scientists can tell the difference between cells. There are many different kinds. Each kind of cell has a different function. Cells with the same function come together to form body tissues and organs. Each cell contains genetic information in the form of deoxyribonucleic acid (DNA). DNA is like a set of instructions that tells the cell what kind of cell it is, what it should do, and where in the body it should be. Normal cells make exact copies of themselves. They do this by copying the information that they contain and then splitting in two. DNA also tells a cell when to grow and divide into new cells and when to stop.

Some cells in the body are not normal. Cancer cells, for example, are abnormal cells that grow out of control. Damaged cells usually repair themselves or "self-destruct." However, cancer cells do not do this. They multiply to form more abnormal cells. Normal, healthy cells divide in an orderly way, but cancer cells reproduce without order. The cancerous cells can form excess tissue masses called tumors. Bone cancer occurs when abnormal cells grow in the bones.

UNDERSTANDING BONES

There are 206 bones in the adult human body. Bones serve many different purposes. One of their functions is to support the body. The bones in the legs, the spinal column, and the pelvis (the bowl-shaped ring of bone at the bottom of the spine) help to support the body. Without bones, people would look a lot like jellyfish. Bones also keep organs safe from injury. Rib bones, for example, protect the lungs, and skull bones protect the brain. Bones fit together, forming joints so that the body can move. Bones also produce red blood cells and white blood cells. Red blood cells carry oxygen throughout the body. White blood cells are infection-fighting cells. The blood cells are made in the soft inside of the bone called the bone marrow.

Bones are lightweight yet extremely strong and hard, due to their structure. Bones are made up of three types of tissue: compact tissue, cancellous tissue, and subchondral tissue. Compact tissue is the hard outer part of most bones. Cancellous tissue makes up the spongy tissue inside the bones, which contains the bone marrow. Subchondral tissue is smooth bone tissue that is found in joints. A layer of cartilage covers

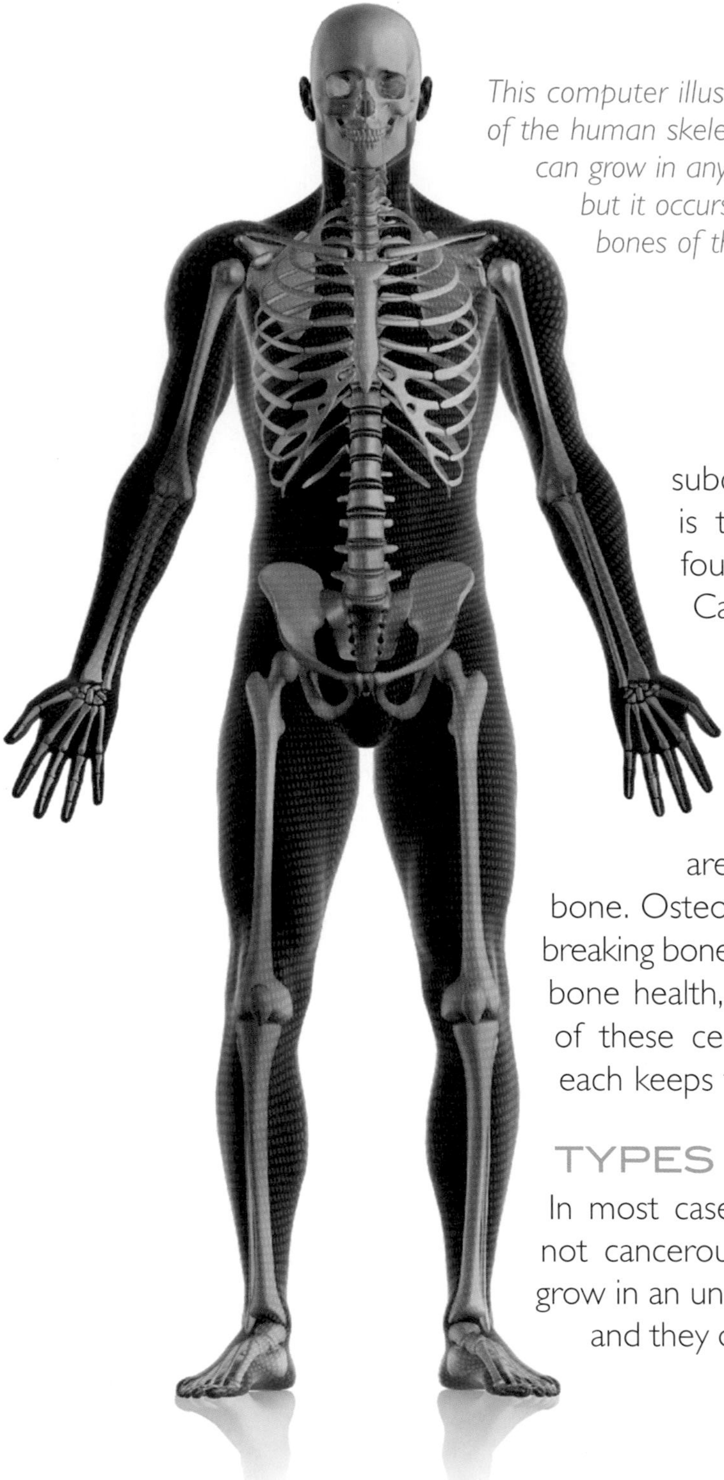

This computer illustration shows the bones of the human skeleton. Primary bone cancer can grow in any of the bones of the body, but it occurs most often in the long bones of the arms and legs.

subchondral tissue. Cartilage is the flexible tissue that is found in the ears and nose. Cartilage acts to cushion the movement of joints.

There are two types of cells inside bone: osteoblasts and osteoclasts. Osteoblasts are responsible for making bone. Osteoclasts are responsible for breaking bone down. To maintain proper bone health, it is important that each of these cells does its job and that each keeps the other in balance.

TYPES OF TUMORS

In most cases, tumors are benign, or not cancerous. These tumors do not grow in an unlimited, aggressive manner, and they do not invade surrounding

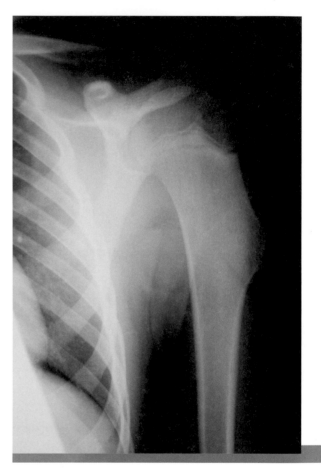

This X-ray shows an osteochondroma of an adolescent boy. The tumor is seen as a lump on the humerus (upper arm bone).

tissues. Benign tumors can usually be removed, and they tend not to grow back. Most benign tumors are harmless to the health of the person. The most common type of benign bone tumors are osteochondromas. Osteochondromas generally occur in people between the ages of ten and twenty. Some benign tumors go away on their own. Other benign tumors can be surgically removed if they cause pain. Though benign bone tumors are rarely life threatening, certain ones are considered risk factors for the development of harmful growths called malignant bone tumors.

Malignant tumor cells can invade and destroy nearby healthy tissues. Unlike benign tumor cells, they are able to travel through the lymph and blood vessels to other parts of the body. Similar to the way that blood vessels transport blood, lymph vessels transport lymph throughout the body. Lymph is a colorless fluid that contains white blood cells and debris—things that the body has recognized as foreign and is trying to eliminate.

After traveling through the body, malignant cancer cells can start new tumors in other areas of the body. This process is called metastasis. When a cancer spreads in this way, it is said to have metastasized. Death may occur when the metastasis cannot be stopped. The cancerous cells take the place of the healthy cells. This causes organ systems to fail, leaving the body unable to properly function. Though tumor cells may spread to other parts of the body, the type of cancer is the same as the original growth. So, if cancer were to spread from the bones to the lungs, it would still be considered bone cancer.

PRIMARY VS. METASTATIC BONE CANCER

The two main types of cancers that are found in the bone are primary bone cancer and metastatic bone cancer. Primary bone cancer is cancer that originally forms on or around the tissues of the bone. Metastatic bone cancer, on the other hand, is cancer that starts in other parts of the body and spreads to the bone. Metastatic bone cancer is one of the most common cancers in the United States. In the late stages of some cancers, cancer cells can leave the primary area and travel to the bone. Metastatic bone cancer usually spreads to the bone from the lungs, the breasts, and the prostate. However, cancer cells that end up in the bone still look like the cancer cells from the organ in which they started. For example, prostate cancer cells that have traveled to the bone do not look like bone cancer cells. They still look like prostate cancer cells. Therefore, the cancer would still be considered prostate cancer and would be treated as such.

Most of the time, when adults have cancer in their bones, it is metastatic bone cancer. Primary bone cancer is much less common.

A colored X-ray shows secondary bone cancer in an arm bone. The cancer, shown in purple, spread from its primary site in the thyroid, a gland in the neck.

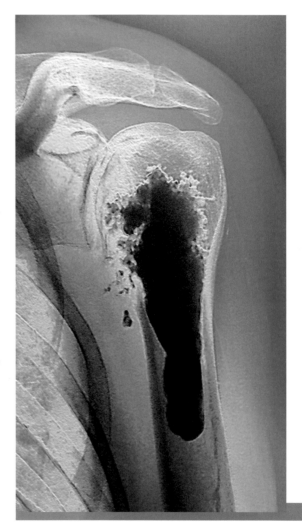

In fact, primary bone cancer accounts for less than 0.2 percent of all cancers and tends to occur mostly in adolescents and young adults. It is important for doctors to determine whether cancer found in the bone originated there or spread from somewhere else. This allows them to determine the proper treatment. Though primary bone cancer is rare, it is considered to be true bone cancer. This book focuses on primary bone cancers.

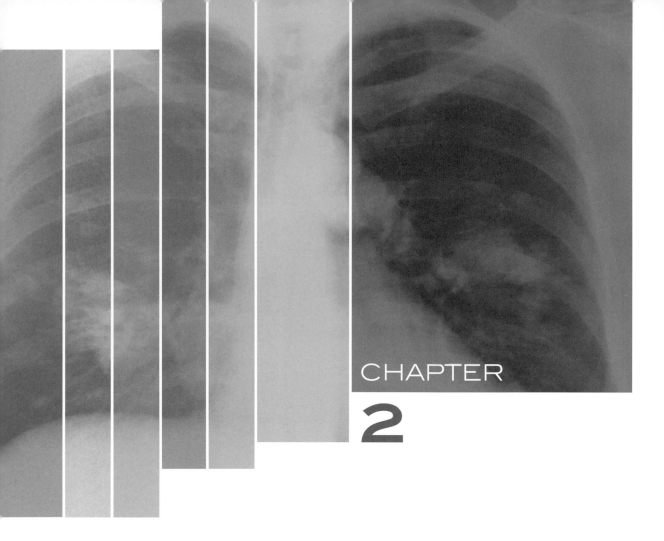

TYPES OF BONE CANCER

Cancer that starts in the bone (primary bone cancer) is rare. However, many people diagnosed with bone cancer will die from the disease. According to the National Cancer Institute, there will be about 2,380 new cases of bone cancer in 2008. An estimated 1,470 of these patients will die. Bone cancer can affect people of any age, but about 30 percent of cases develop in children and teenagers.

Most malignant bone cancers are called sarcomas. Sarcomas are cancers that begin in the connective tissue. This is tissue such as bone that supports other body parts. The most common primary bone cancers are: osteosarcoma, chondrosarcoma, Ewing sarcoma, chordoma, and malignant fibrosarcoma.

OSTEOSARCOMA

Osteosarcoma (also called osteogenic sarcoma) is the most common type of bone cancer. It tends to affect adolescents. Osteosarcoma accounts for about 35 percent of primary bone cancer cases. About nine hundred new cases of osteosarcoma are diagnosed in the United States each year. The majority of those affected are young. In fact, about 60 percent of people who develop osteosarcoma are between the ages of ten and thirty. Another 10 percent of cases occur in people between the ages of sixty and seventy.

Osteosarcoma usually develops from osteoblasts—the cells responsible for bone growth. For this reason, osteosarcoma is often seen in teens who are undergoing growth spurts. Studies show that boys are twice as likely as girls to develop osteosarcoma. Osteosarcoma especially seems to affect boys who are on the taller end of the spectrum. It affects adolescents and young adults of all ethnicities. Osteosarcoma is most often found in the bones around the knee or shoulder, but it can occur in other bones as well.

The symptoms of osteosarcoma include pain and swelling in the arm or leg. Usually, the pain and swelling occur in the longer bones of the body, like the upper arm bone near the shoulder or the lower leg bone below the knee. The pain may worsen at night and may wake the person. The pain may also worsen during exercise. At times, the symptoms of osteosarcoma are mistaken for a sports injury such as a sprain. This is particularly the case with active teenagers. In some cases, the first sign of osteosarcoma is a broken arm or leg bone. This happens because the cancer has weakened the bone by crowding out and replacing normal bone cells.

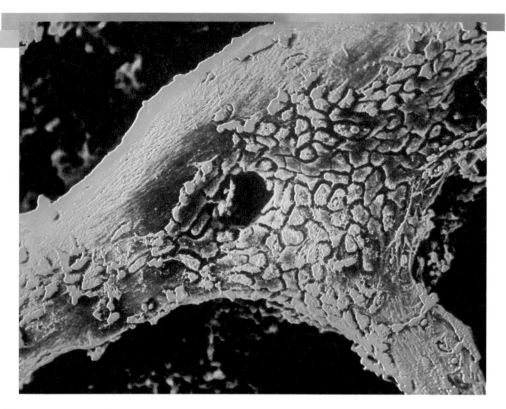

This illustration shows osteoblast cells on a section of bone, forming new bone tissue. Most osteosarcomas develop from osteoblasts.

CHONDROSARCOMA

Chondrosarcoma is the second most common primary bone cancer. It accounts for about 26 percent of the cases of primary bone cancers. Chondrosarcoma arises from cells in the cartilage. Cartilage is a strong, elastic tissue that is softer than bone. It provides support, flexibility, and elasticity to the skeleton in places throughout the body. Most bone forms from cartilage. First the cartilage forms, and then calcium is

A colored X-ray shows a bone affected by chondrosarcoma. This type of bone cancer begins from cells in cartilage, in this case the cartilage at the head of the femur (upper leg bone).

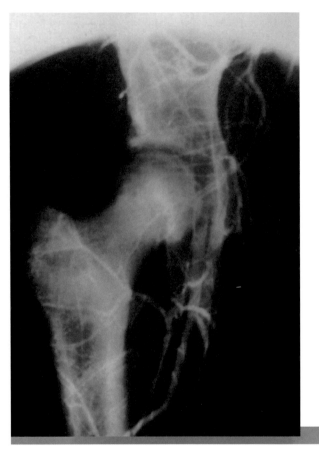

deposited on it to form the bone. The skeleton of a fetus, or unborn baby, is mainly made up of cartilage. Most cartilage is replaced by bone as a person grows, but some of it remains into adulthood. In adults, cartilage is found in the rib cage, the ears, the nose, the airways to and within the lungs, and the discs between vertebrae. Intervertebral discs serve as cushions between the bones of the spine. Cartilage also remains at the ends of bones, where it acts as a cushion between the bones.

Chondrosarcoma can develop anywhere in the body where cartilage is present. It typically forms in the upper arms and legs and the pelvic and shoulder bones. However, chondrosarcoma can be found in any bone of the body, including the base of the skull. Chondrosarcoma can occur at any age, but it is most commonly found in people between the ages of forty and seventy. Men and women seem to be equally affected by it.

The symptoms of chondrosarcoma vary depending on where in the body the tumor is located. One symptom is a large mass on the affected bone. There may be pressure around the mass. A person may experience pain from chondrosarcoma for years before he or she is diagnosed. However, the pain gradually increases over time. Usually, the pain is worse at night and is not relieved with rest.

EWING SARCOMA

Ewing sarcoma is the third most common type of bone cancer, accounting for 16 percent of the cases. Ewing sarcoma was named for the doctor who first described it, Dr. James Ewing. No one is entirely sure what the cell of origin is for Ewing sarcoma. It most likely originates in soft tissues and always invades bone. Very rarely, Ewing sarcoma occurs in soft tissues only, instead of bone. Soft tissue includes fat, muscle, and deep skin tissue. When Ewing sarcoma affects soft tissue only, it is called extraosseous Ewing sarcoma. (*Extraosseous* means "outside the bone.") Under a microscope, the cells of Ewing sarcoma appear small, round, and blue.

Ewing sarcoma mainly affects children and adolescents. It is usually found in people between the ages of ten and twenty, but it may occur in those up to thirty years old. About two hundred children and teenagers in the United States are diagnosed with Ewing sarcoma each year. Ewing sarcoma is more common in boys. It also occurs more frequently in Caucasians and is rare among African Americans and Asian Americans. In fact, more than 80 percent of patients affected with Ewing sarcoma are white. Ewing sarcoma can occur in any bone in the body, but it is most often found in the pelvis, the thigh, the lower leg, the upper arm, and the ribs. The exact cause of Ewing sarcoma is unknown. It may be related to rapid bone growth, which would explain why Ewing sarcoma is frequently seen in growing teenagers.

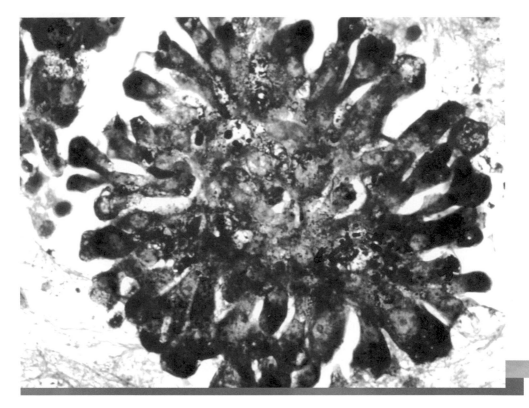

This illustration shows metastasized Ewing sarcoma cells. They have been stained to show up better under the microscope.

About 60 percent of Ewing sarcoma in the bone causes swelling. Often, the tumor is warm and soft to the touch. Most people suffering from Ewing sarcoma also experience bone pain. This pain may be caused by the spread of the tumor in the bone. It may also be caused by a fracture in a bone that has been weakened by the tumor. Another symptom of Ewing sarcoma is fever. Ewing sarcoma may initially be mistaken for a simple bone bruise or a bone infection. It may only be after antibiotics have failed to help that a child is diagnosed with Ewing sarcoma. This cancer can spread to the lungs, other bones, and

DR. JAMES EWING

Dr. James Ewing was born on December 25, 1866, in Pittsburgh, Pennsylvania. In 1888, Ewing began attending the College of Physicians and Surgeons of New York. Later, he was given an internship at the Roosevelt Hospital and Sloane Maternity in New York. It was here that he developed an interest in pathology, which is the study of disease. Ewing published his first book, *Clinical Pathology of Blood*, in 1901. In 1902, he helped to establish the P. Huntington Fund for Cancer Research. He later cofounded both the American Association for Cancer Research in 1907 and the American Society for the Control of Cancer (now known as the American Cancer Society) in 1913. In 1920, he presented a paper on the malignant bone sarcoma that would later be named for him. Ewing played a large role in the development of cancer research. In 1943, at the age of seventy-six, he died of bladder cancer. More than a thousand people attended his funeral.

bone marrow. The patient may experience fatigue (tiredness) and weight loss. If the tumor is growing near the spine, then the patient may also experience paralysis. This is very rare, however.

CHORDOMA
Chordoma is a rare form of bone cancer, accounting for about 8 percent of bone cancers. It most often occurs in the spine. Chordoma usually develops from the notochord, a rod made of cartilage that forms the early spine in a fetus as it grows in the womb. After about the sixth month of development, most of the notochord has been replaced by

the bones of the spine. Small amounts of the notochord may remain, however. These can sometimes develop into chordoma. Chordoma can occur anywhere in the spine, but most often it develops at the bottom of the spine or at the base of the skull. Though chordoma can develop at any age, most people are between forty and sixty years old when they are diagnosed. It is very rare for a child to develop chordoma.

Chordoma grows very slowly and doesn't usually spread to other parts of the body. Because it takes a long time to develop, chordoma can be difficult to diagnose. The symptoms of chordoma include constipation, bleeding from the rectum, numbness, headaches, facial pain, double vision, changes in hearing, and difficulty swallowing.

FIBROSARCOMA AND MALIGNANT FIBROUS HISTIOCYTOMA

Fibrosarcoma and malignant fibrous histiocytoma are cancers that usually develop in soft tissues. However, these rare cancers do sometimes start in the bones. They account for about 6 percent of bone cancers. When they do develop in the bones, they usually affect the legs, arms, and jaw. Malignant fibrous histiocytoma grows rather quickly and often spreads to other parts of the body, usually the lymph nodes and the lungs. Fibrosarcoma and malignant fibrous histiocytoma are rare among children. These cancers usually occur in elderly and middle-aged adults.

GIANT CELL TUMOR OF THE BONE

Giant cell tumor (GCT) of the bone is a fairly rare cancer. Giant cell tumors are named by the way they look under the microscope. These giant cells form when many cells come together to form a large, single complex. GCT has both benign and malignant forms. The benign (non-cancerous) form is more common. GCT is only malignant about 10 percent of the time. However, when a giant cell tumor is removed, it

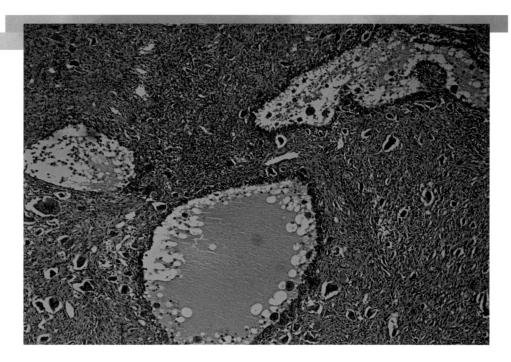

Above is a section of a giant cell tumor (GCT). Giant cell tumors develop when many cells come together to form a complex. Most giant cell tumors are benign.

often grows back in the same place that it first occurred. When it grows back, GCT is more likely to spread to other parts of the body. This cancer often affects the leg (usually near the knee) or the arm bones. Giant cell tumor of the bone most often occurs in people between the ages of twenty and forty. It is rarely seen in children or in adults over the age of sixty-five.

The first symptom of GCT is usually pain in the area of the tumor. This pain generally starts out mild, but it increases over time. There may also be pain when a nearby joint is moved. The pain usually increases with activity and decreases with rest. Occasionally, the bone is weakened and breaks. Sometimes, a patient will notice a mass but will feel no pain.

MYTHS AND FACTS

MYTH Only old people get bone cancer.

FACT Two of the three most common types of bone cancer—osteosarcoma and Ewing sarcoma—tend to appear in adolescents.

MYTH All tumors are malignant (cancerous).

FACT The majority of tumors are actually benign. Benign tumors usually do not grow out of control, and they do not invade surrounding tissue.

MYTH A diagnosis of bone cancer means automatic amputation of the affected limb.

FACT Sometimes, amputation is required to treat bone cancer. However, with improvements in surgical techniques and therapies like chemotherapy and radiation, amputation is much less common than it was in the past.

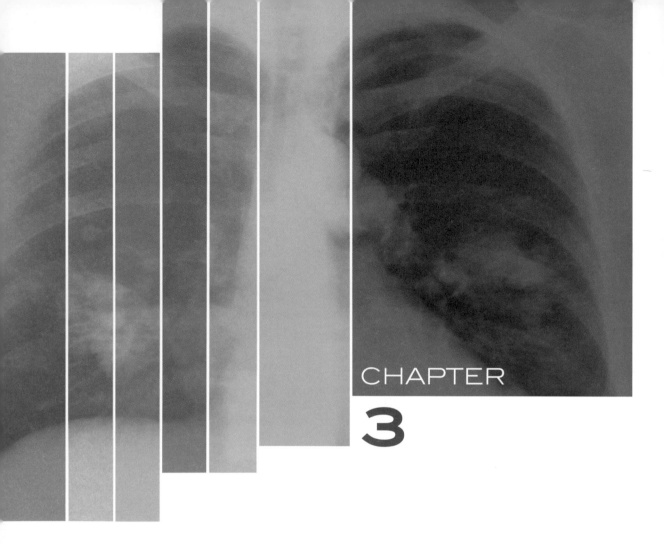

WHO GETS BONE CANCER?

The exact cause of bone cancer is not known. Doctors can seldom say why one person gets bone cancer and another does not. However, it is known that cancer is not contagious. A person cannot catch it from someone else. Though an exact cause is not known, bone cancer research has uncovered many risk factors for developing the disease. Risk factors are anything that increases a person's chances of developing a certain disease.

Risk factors could be a person's age, family history, diet, or behaviors. Every disease has different risk factors. Smoking, for example, is a risk factor for developing lung cancer. Exposing skin to strong sunlight is a risk factor for developing skin cancer. However, having risk factors for a particular disease does not necessarily mean that a person will develop that disease. People with several risk factors for a disease may never get it, while someone with no risk factors may.

Knowing risk factors can help a person to make informed decisions about his or her behavior. A person who is at risk for developing a certain disease can also be monitored by health care professionals. Some of the risk factors for developing bone cancer are: age, gender, race, genetics, exposure to radiation, a history of benign bone tumors, and the presence of other bone diseases. It is important to remember that most people with bone cancer do not have any known risk factors. Researchers are still working to figure out the causes.

AGE, GENDER, AND RACE

For good reason, most people think of cancer as a disease of the elderly. More than 70 percent of cancers affect people who are over the age of sixty. However, there are some cancers that are more likely to affect young people. One example is leukemia. This is a cancer of the white blood cells. Another cancer that is more common among the young is testicular cancer. Testicular cancer is cancer of the testes, which are part of the male reproductive system where sperm is produced. Though some bone cancers are more common in older people, the majority of bone cancer sufferers are children and teenagers. Both osteosarcoma and Ewing sarcoma are more common among the young. Since most teens that are affected by bone cancer are taller than their peers, many experts feel there is a relationship between rapid bone growth and bone cancer.

Gender is another factor in the development of bone cancer. Osteo-sarcoma and Ewing sarcoma are both more common among males. In fact, osteosarcoma is almost twice as common among males as females.

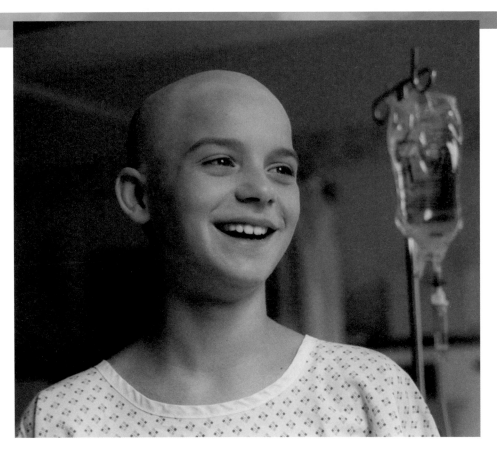

Though cancer mainly affects older people, some cancers are more likely to affect young people, like this boy. The majority of bone cancer sufferers are children and teenagers.

This could be due to the rapid rate at which adolescent boys grow. Osteosarcoma occurs in all races. However, it occurs slightly more in African Americans than in Caucasians. Ewing sarcoma, on the other hand, is most common in Caucasians, then in Latinos, and then (quite rarely) in African Americans and Asian Americans.

GENETICS

A very small percentage of bone cancers (usually osteosarcoma) seem to be hereditary. This means the cancer is passed from one generation to the next through genes, or DNA. Genes are the basic units that determine the traits, or characteristics, that people inherit from their parents. There are some rare inherited cancer syndromes that increase a

Some inherited cancer syndromes increase a child's risk for developing certain bone cancers, such as osteosarcoma. These syndromes are passed down in families from one generation to the next.

child's risk of developing bone cancer. One is called Li-Fraumeni syndrome. With Li-Fraumeni syndrome, a mutation of a certain gene called p53 is passed from parents to offspring. A mutation is a change in a gene that results in a new trait being passed down. The gene that is mutated is one that helps to control the growth and division of cells. Such a gene would normally keep tumors from growing.

Another inherited syndrome that increases a child's likelihood of developing bone cancer is called Rothmund-Thompson syndrome. This disorder involves the mutation of a gene that is responsible for making a certain protein called a helicase. Helicases are vital to the normal copying of DNA and the repair of damaged DNA. They help to make sure that the DNA has no errors. A person with this mutation would have widespread damage to his or her genetic information. Therefore, a person with Rothmund-Thompson syndrome suffers from many physical problems. These include skin, nail, teeth, and eye problems, as well as underdeveloped or missing sexual organs, baldness, and short stature. Children with Rothmund-Thompson syndrome are also at an increased risk for developing skin cancer and bone cancer (usually osteosarcoma).

Multiple hereditary exostoses (MHE) is another inherited condition that increases a person's risk for bone cancer. MHE causes bumps—called exostoses or osteochondromas—to form on the bones. About 40 percent of people affected with MHE are affected before the age of ten. The growths can form on any bone, but they most often grow on the legs, arms, fingers, toes, pelvis, and shoulder blades. These bumps can be painful and can cause the bones to deform or break. Exostoses can be especially painful for growing kids. Patients with MHE have an increased risk of developing both osteosarcoma and chondrosarcoma.

Another disease that can put children at risk for developing bone cancer is retinoblastoma. This is a rare eye cancer that affects children, usually in infancy and during the toddler years. Between 6 and 10 percent of the cases of retinoblastoma are inherited. Children who have the inherited form of retinoblastoma are at a greater risk for later developing osteosarcoma.

RADIATION

It is thought that most genetic mutations that put people at risk for developing bone cancer are not inherited. Instead, they are mutations that occur during a person's life. Exposure to large doses of radiation may increase a person's risk for developing bone cancer. Radiation is a type of energy. Some forms of radiant energy can penetrate the body. X-rays are one example. However, the exposure to radiation that people get from X-rays won't harm them. The amount of radiation used during an X-ray is only about ten times the amount of radiation that people are exposed to naturally each day. It may surprise you to learn that people are exposed to radiation from natural sources all the time. For example, radiation comes from the sun, from outer space, and even from the ground and rocks.

People are exposed to larger doses of radiation when they receive radiation therapy to treat cancer. Radiation therapy uses high-energy radiation to kill cancer cells. This high level of radiation exposure puts people at risk for developing other cancers, especially if they receive the therapy when they are young or if the radiation dose is high. It is rare, but when bones cells are exposed to radiation during treatment for other cancers, they could become cancerous themselves. However, radiation exposure more often leads to blood-related cancers (leukemia or lymphoma) than to bone cancers.

Radiation therapy is becoming more sophisticated. Doctors are increasingly better able to target the tumor being treated. Such advances may lead to fewer cases of bone cancer arising from the treatment of other cancers.

A chest X-ray exposes the patient to small amounts of radiation. Large amounts of radiation can be dangerous to one's health. However, studies have consistently shown that the dose of radiation used in X-rays does not cause cancer.

RADIOACTIVE WATCHES

Exposure to radioactive materials such as radium and strontium can cause bone cancer. Radioactive substances give off energy in the form of a stream of particles. Exposure to this energy is damaging and can be fatal.

In the 1920s, radium paint was used to make the dials of watches glow. As workers painted the watch dials, they would touch their paintbrushes to their tongues so that their brushes would form a point. As they did this, the workers were taking in high doses of radium, which collected in their bones. In the years that followed, a huge number of these workers developed bone cancer. Later research confirmed the cancer-causing effects of exposure to radium.

BENIGN BONE TUMORS

Occasionally, bone cancer can arise from benign (non-cancerous) bone or cartilage tumors. Osteochondromas can slightly increase a person's risk for bone cancer. They are benign tumors that are formed by bone and cartilage. Osteochondromas are the most common type of tumors in children. Each osteochondroma has a slight risk of developing into osteosarcoma or chondrosarcoma. Most osteochondromas, however, can easily be surgically removed. Some people inherit a tendency to have multiple osteochondromas. Because it is difficult to remove all of the osteochondromas, these people have an increased risk for developing osteosarcoma or chondrosarcoma.

Others with a higher risk for developing chondrosarcoma are people with multiple enchondromas. However, it is not very likely that

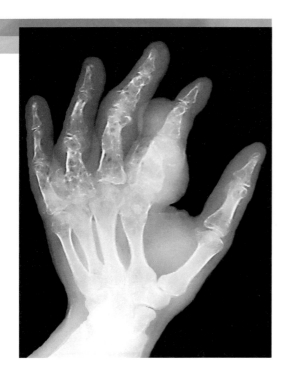

This X-ray shows a hand with multiple enchondroma tumors. They appear as lobe-shaped white tumors in the middle of the bone.

enchondroma will turn into cancerous chondrosarcoma. Enchondroma is a type of benign tumor of the cartilage that appears on the inside of the bone. These tumors usually begin during childhood. They are often found in people between the ages of ten and twenty. These benign tumors usually occur in the small bones of the hands or feet. In fact, enchondroma is the most common type of tumor in the hand. Though a single enchondroma can become cancerous, it is very rare. People with multiple enchondromas are at a much greater risk.

OTHER BONE DISEASE

Experts feel that people who have had other bone diseases, like Paget's disease, are at an increased risk of developing bone cancer later on. Paget's disease of the bone affects the normal growth process of bones. About 5 to 10 percent of people who have had severe cases of Paget's disease develop osteosarcoma.

Bones constantly break down and reform throughout one's life. With Paget's disease, bone breaks down at an increased rate. When the bone grows back, it is softer than normal. Paget's disease can affect any bone in the body, but it usually affects the hips, the skull, the legs, the back, and the pelvic bone. The affected bones sometimes become shorter, but they can also grow larger than before. Bones affected with Paget's disease are weaker than normal bone and break more easily. The exact cause of Paget's disease is not known. Some scientists believe that it is hereditary. Studies have shown that as many as 30 percent of people with Paget's disease have other family members who also have it. Others believe that it might be caused by a slow-acting virus. Paget's disease seems to affect men more than women. It usually affects people who are over the age of forty.

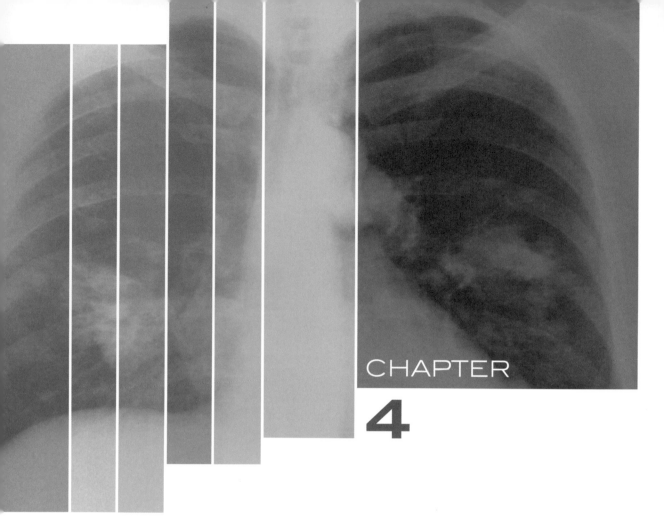

DIAGNOSING BONE CANCER

Currently, there is no way to prevent bone cancer. Early detection and treatment offer a patient the best hope. People who have risk factors for bone cancer and are experiencing symptoms should visit their doctors. The first thing a doctor will usually do is ask a patient questions about his or her personal medical history and the medical histories of family members. It is important for doctors to find out if anyone in a patient's family has had cancer. Next, a doctor will perform a physical examination of the patient. During the physical exam, a doctor may be able to feel a

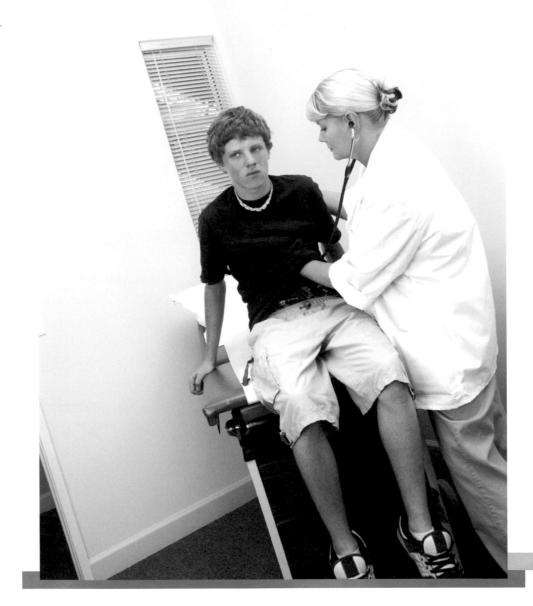

Routine physical examinations are important for the early detection of health problems such as bone cancer.

tumor if one is present. If a doctor suspects bone cancer, then further tests will be arranged. These tests will help the doctor to determine the best treatment for the patient.

LABORATORY TESTS

When cancer is suspected, blood and urine tests are some of the first tests that a doctor will perform. There is no single blood test that can prove the presence or absence of cancer, but a complete blood test can help to guide a doctor's diagnosis. Blood and urine tests give a doctor clues about what is going on in a patient's body. Doctors look for different substances in blood and urine to find out whether a person's organs are functioning properly. For instance, excess waste products in the blood could indicate that the kidneys are not working properly. Also, cancer cells give off substances called tumor markers, which can be detected in blood and urine. Large amounts of the enzyme alkaline phosphatase in the blood could indicate bone cancer. (However, it is important to know that large amounts of this enzyme are normally present when a child is growing or when a broken bone is mending.) Blood in the urine could also be evidence of cancer, but it could also be a sign of many other, less serious problems. Though blood and urine tests can give doctors clues, additional tests are usually needed to make a diagnosis.

IMAGING TESTS

Imaging tests create pictures of the bones, organs, and internal tissues. These tests allow doctors to better examine an area of concern. They help doctors to locate tumors, determine how far the cancer has progressed, and make sure treatment is working once it has begun. For bone cancer, imaging tests include X-rays, bone scans, computed tomography (CT) scans, magnetic resonance imaging (MRI), positron emission tomography (PET) scans, and, occasionally, ultrasounds.

X-rays are fairly inexpensive, quick, and painless, so they are usually one of the first tests performed. X-rays use high-energy radiation, which passes through the body. As it does, it creates shadows on a sheet of film. On the film, soft tissue appears dark and bone appears white. This is because the energy from the X-ray is able to pass through the soft tissue much more easily. On X-ray film, tumors may either appear as very dark areas or very white ones, depending on how solid they are. Doctors use X-rays to show the location, size, and shape of bone tumors. Medical professionals have used X-rays for about one hundred years.

Bone scans require a patient to be injected with a small amount of low-level radioactive material, called a tracer. The tracer travels through the blood and gathers in the patient's bones. Once in the body, the tracer gives off radiation that can be detected by a special camera. The patient lies very still on a table while the camera takes pictures of the bones. It is not painful.

Computed tomography (CT) scans use X-rays along with a computer to create thin, clear slices or cross-sectional pictures of the body. CT scans give doctors much more information than X-rays alone. The patient lies flat and still on a table while a scanner rotates around it. The scanner shoots thousands of low-energy X-ray beams at the area that the doctor wants to look at. The X-rays pass through the person and into a detector on the other side. The pictures are displayed on a computer screen. The images clearly show the size, volume, shape, and location of a tumor. A CT scan takes only a few minutes and is painless.

A positron emission tomography (PET) scan is yet another imaging test. During a PET scan, a radioactive form of sugar is injected into the patient. The sugar is taken up by active or growing cells. As cancer cells are very active and multiply very

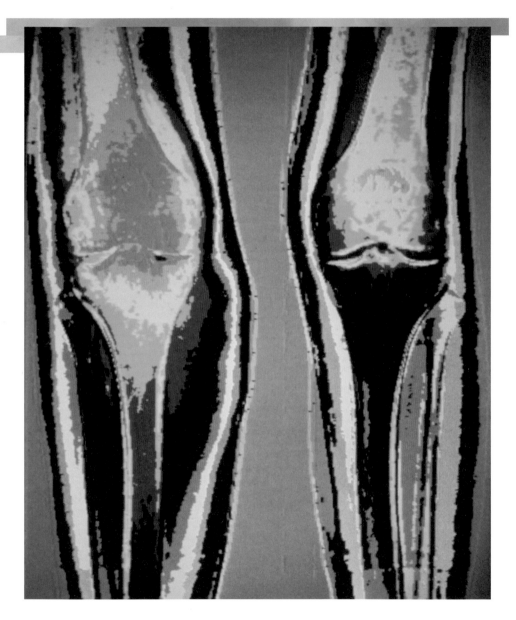

This computed tomography (CT) scan reveals bone cancer on the right leg. Such imaging technology helps doctors make a diagnosis without having to cut open the patient.

quickly, they absorb a lot of the radioactive sugar. During the test, a patient lies on a table inside a large doughnut-shaped chamber. A special camera records the radioactivity leaving the body. The picture shows up on a computer. This test takes about an hour and is painless.

— **Magnetic resonance imaging (MRI)** uses radio waves and very powerful magnets to create a detailed picture of the inside of the body. It is different from other imaging tests because it does not use radiation. The patient lies on a table that moves into a long, metal tunnel. Getting an MRI is painless, but it is very loud. Many people become claustrophobic during an MRI test. Being claustrophobic means that a person feels uncomfortable in an enclosed space. Some facilities now offer "open" MRIs. These machines have open sides and no pounding noise.

BIOPSY

The best way to diagnose cancer is to remove a sample of the tumor and examine it under a microscope. This procedure is called a biopsy. The sample can be removed with a needle biopsy or an incisional biopsy. During needle biopsies, doctors make a small hole in the bone and remove a sample of the tumor with a needle. A numbing medicine is used to prevent pain. Some people (usually children) may be put completely to sleep for the procedure. There are two main kinds of needle biopsies: a fine needle aspiration (FNA) biopsy and a core needle biopsy. Fine needle aspiration biopsy uses a very thin needle to remove individual cells and very small groups of cells. A core needle biopsy uses a thicker needle to remove a cylinder-shaped mass of tissue. The core needle biopsy provides a larger and better sample to be studied.

For an incisional biopsy, a doctor cuts through the patient's skin and removes a large piece of the suspicious tissue. The biopsy may be done

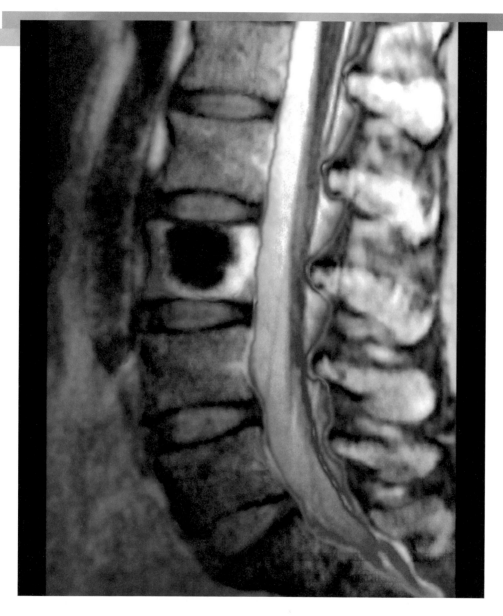

Here, an MRI scan shows secondary bone cancer of the spine. MRIs use radio waves and strong magnetic fields to produce detailed images of bones and organs inside a person's body.

This bone biopsy sample is held in a pair of tweezers. Biopsies like this one are analyzed to diagnose bone cancer.

in a doctor's office, a surgical facility, or a hospital. This depends on the location and size of the tumor, how much tumor needs to be removed, and the way the tissue is to be removed.

The tissue that is removed during a biopsy is examined by a doctor whose specialty is identifying diseases by studying cells and tissues under a microscope. This specialist, called a pathologist, can determine whether the tumor is benign or malignant. If the tumor is malignant, then the next step is to determine if it is primary or metastatic bone cancer. Pathologists can also tell the doctor exactly which type of bone cancer they are dealing with. With the information doctors gather from tests, it is possible to determine the stage of bone cancer as well.

BONE CANCER GRADING AND STAGING

The stage of bone cancer tells how far the disease has spread. Doctors need to determine the stage of bone cancer in order to come up with the best plan of treatment. The system that doctors usually use to stage bone cancer is the American Joint Commission on Cancer (AJCC) system. In this system, "T" represents the size of the tumor, "N" stands for the spread to the lymph nodes, "M" is for metastasis (spread) to distant parts of the body, and "G" stands for the grade of the tumor.

Doctors grade cancer cells according to how they look under the microscope. Cancer cells that look more abnormal are more likely to be aggressive. The two grades for bone cancer cells are high- and low-grade. The more abnormal cells are called high-grade. If the bone cancer cells don't look that different from normal bone cells, then they are low-grade. A low-grade bone cancer is less aggressive and less likely to spread. During staging, numbers are added to each of the letters from the AJCC system. These numbers describe the size of the tumor and the extent to which the cancer has spread. Doctors use this staging process to determine the best treatment options for their patients. Below is a general outline of the AJCC Staging System.

T Stages of Bone Cancer (Tumor Size)

T0: No evidence of a tumor
T1: Tumor is around 3 inches (8 centimeters) or less in diameter
T2: Tumor is larger than around 3 inches in diameter
T3: Tumor has moved to another site or sites on the same bone

N Stages of Bone Cancer (Lymph Nodes)

N0: No spread to nearby lymph nodes
N1: The cancer has spread to nearby lymph nodes

M Stages of Bone Cancer (Metastasis)

M0: No metastasis

M1: Distant metastasis

M1a: Cancer has spread only to the lung(s)

M1b: Cancer has spread to other sites

Grades of Bone Cancer

G1–G2: Low-grade

G3–G4: High-grade

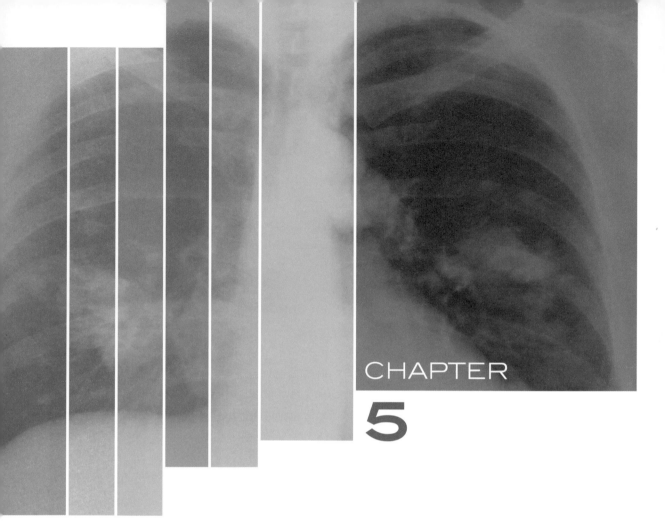

TREATMENT FOR BONE CANCER

After a patient is diagnosed with bone cancer, the next step in the process is for doctors to lay out a plan for treatment. Treatment for bone cancer is based on several factors. What type of bone cancer is it? What stage is the cancer in? Where is the tumor located and how big is it? What are the age and general health of the patient? Answers to these questions will help a doctor to decide the best course of treatment. The three main types of treatment for bone cancer are surgery, radiation therapy, and chemotherapy. Most patients need a combination of these treatments.

SURGERY

Surgery is the most common treatment for bone cancer. It is generally performed after several cycles of chemotherapy have been used in an attempt to shrink the tumor first. (This is called neo-adjuvant chemotherapy.) Surgery for non-metastatic cancer involves removing the tumor and a portion of healthy bone surrounding it. Years ago, amputation—the removal of the affected limb—was very common when treating bone cancer. Today, medical advances have allowed doctors to perform limb-sparing surgeries on many bone cancer patients. Limb-sparing surgery involves the diseased portion of the bone being removed. Then, the gap created by the missing bone is filled in with either an endoprosthesis (an internal prosthetic) or a bone graft. A bone graft can be a portion of bone from another part of the patient's body or from another person. When a limb-sparing operation is performed, doctors do their best not to disturb the rest of the limb, while still completely removing the tumor. Surgeons work carefully so that they do not harm nerves, tendons, ligaments, and blood vessels. These are all needed to keep the limb working.

In the past, using surgery to treat children with bone cancer was tricky. Children grow, but the metal rods that were being used to replace their diseased bones did not grow with them. As a consequence, doctors had to perform multiple surgeries to lengthen the prosthetic limb. In the mid-1980s, however, expandable prosthetics were invented. These have now been improved to the point that the devices can be extended without additional surgery.

Surgeons have also gotten much better at replacing diseased bone with bone from another part of the body. They are now regularly able to reconnect bone, blood vessels, and, most important, the growth plate. The growth plate is the area of growing tissue in the bones of

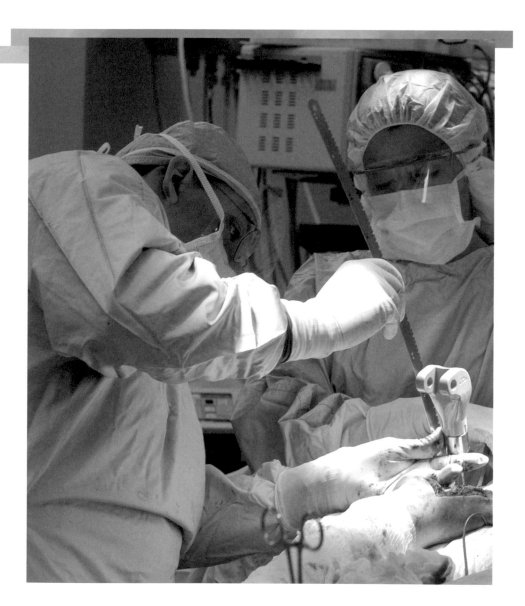

Surgeons remove the diseased portion of bone from a six-year-old bone cancer victim. The bone will be replaced with the Repiphysis expandable implant. This young boy will require no further surgery to lengthen the device as he grows.

children and adolescents. Bone moved from another location should grow on its own, requiring no further surgery.

Sometimes, however, a doctor has no choice but to amputate part or all of an affected limb in order to fight the cancer. Amputation is necessary when the tumor has extended into blood vessels or nerves, or when the tumor is so big that a limb-sparing procedure is not possible. When performing an amputation, surgeons purposely leave extra muscle and skin around the end of the limb. This allows the patient to later be fitted with a prosthesis, or artificial limb. Losing a limb can be very upsetting, especially for active teenagers. Counseling and physical therapy can help a teen deal with this change. Most teens with prosthetics are able to return to their normal activities, including sports.

Major improvements in prosthetic technology over the last thirty years have made them lighter-weight and stronger. Prosthetics that used to be made from wood and metal are now made out of advanced plastics and carbon fiber. Carbon fiber is plastic that is reinforced with carbon fibers. This combination results in a very strong, yet lightweight material. New materials are also used to make a more natural-looking artificial "skin" to cover prosthetics. The use of microchips has led to advanced prosthetics. Computerized, self-adjusting knees and ankles, for example, are able to adapt to changes in the ground that their users are walking on. Artificial knees are also able to actively power their wearers up stairs and steep slopes. Artificial hands are being made that contain sensors in the fingertips to monitor the force of the user's grip.

RADIATION THERAPY

Radiation therapy uses high-energy radiation to kill bone cancer cells. The radiation damages the DNA in the cells, causing them to die. Cancer cells are more likely to be affected by the radiation because they divide more rapidly. However, some healthy cells are also destroyed during radiation therapy.

*When limb amputation is necessary, a patient can be fitted with a prosthesis.
A good prosthesis allows a person to engage in most normal activities.*

With external radiation therapy, a large machine points a beam of radiation at the affected area. This type of radiation treatment does not require a hospital stay. The patient goes to the hospital to receive treatment when necessary, but he or she can go home that same day. Radiation therapy is painless, although it does cause some side effects. The most common ones are tiredness, nausea, and loss of appetite. Osteosarcoma is not very sensitive to radiation therapy, so this type of

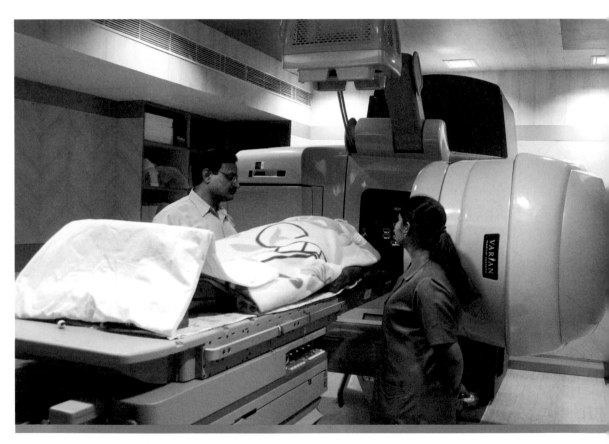

Radiologists in South Asia use a high-tech image guided radiation therapy (IGRT) machine. IGRT reduces the amount of healthy tissue exposed to radiation by more accurately directing the radiation to a certain location on a patient.

treatment is not often used to treat it. Ewing sarcoma, on the other hand, responds well to radiation therapy. When treating bone cancer, radiation therapy is often used in conjunction with surgery and chemotherapy.

CHEMOTHERAPY

Chemotherapy, often simply referred to as "chemo," is a type of treatment that uses chemicals or drugs to kill cancer cells. Some drugs are injected intravenously (into a vein), while others are given orally (by mouth). Radiation therapy and surgery concentrate treatment on a specific (local) area; chemotherapy, on the other hand, destroys cancer cells throughout the body. Chemotherapy drugs work by disrupting rapidly dividing cells, including cancer cells. However, they also affect other normal cells that divide rapidly. For instance, hair follicles, reproductive cells, and the cells lining the digestive tract all grow quickly. Therefore, these cells are also affected by chemotherapy. This explains the hair loss, infertility, and vomiting associated with chemotherapy. Infertility means that a person is unable to have children. Some chemotherapy drugs (but not all) can cause infertility.

Chemo is used throughout the bone cancer treatment process, and it is usually used in conjunction with radiation therapy and surgery. Chemotherapy is sometimes used before surgery to shrink a cancer tumor. It is then used after surgery to try to stop the cancer from coming back. Chemotherapy is also used with advanced cancers (those that have spread) to control symptoms and slow down the cancer's growth. Some bone cancers respond very well to chemotherapy.

WHAT THE FUTURE HOLDS

The National Cancer Institute and other organizations like it are dedicated to understanding cancer and finding new and better ways to treat it. Cancer organizations are always conducting clinical trials such as those through the national Children's Oncology Group. Clinical trials are research

OVERCOMING DISABILITY

Today's most determined disabled athletes have revolutionized the world of prosthetics. In an effort to continue with the sports they love, athletes with missing limbs have customized prosthetics that specifically work well for their sports. Sprinters use artificial feet with no heels. There are also special artificial arm attachments for sports such as fishing, bowling, and weightlifting. When Warren Macdonald, a mountain climber, lost both of his legs, he searched for a way to continue with his sport. He helped to design miniature, carbon-fiber climbing legs. These legs were created purposely to keep Macdonald's center of gravity low. When athletes have a low center of gravity, they are more balanced. Macdonald's prosthetic legs

Warren Macdonald's Web site (www. warren-macdonald.com) tells his inspirational story and features books and DVDs about him.

were also spring-loaded so that they could absorb shock. The feet on the end of Macdonald's prosthetics also had boot soles. The rubber-coated feet helped him to get footholds in rocky cliffs. Wearing his prosthetic legs, Macdonald became the first amputee to climb Africa's tallest peak, 19,341-foot Mt. Kilimanjaro.

studies that determine if new medical approaches work in people. Clinical trials are used to find better ways to treat bone cancer. Researchers test the best combinations of surgery, chemotherapy, and radiation, and they also look for new drugs or better combinations of proven drugs.

In recent years, treatment for bone cancer has progressed enormously. As a result, both the life expectancy and the quality of life of bone cancer patients have increased greatly. Advances in surgery and chemotherapy have allowed limbs to be saved about 85 percent of the time. Advances in prosthetics have also increased the quality of life for those patients who must undergo amputation. More advances are expected in the future. Scientists hope that people will someday be able to use prosthetic limbs that will be controlled by a microchip in the brain. These limbs would be able to respond like the original limbs. When the brain thinks about moving the limb, the prosthesis would respond immediately.

Improved chemotherapy, radiation, and surgical techniques have greatly increased the long-term survival of bone cancer patients. Twenty years ago, only about 20 to 30 percent of bone cancer patients survived their battle with the disease. Today, the overall survival rate has increased to about 60 percent. Doctors expect that, with future advances, this number will continue to rise.

TEN GREAT QUESTIONS
TO ASK YOUR ONCOLOGIST

1. What kind of bone cancer do I have?

2. Has there been any spread from the primary site?

3. What stage cancer do I have?

4. What treatment choices are open to me?

5. What are the risks and side effects of each of these treatments?

6. What are the chances of the cancer returning?

7. What is the survival rate for this type and stage of bone cancer?

8. What is my prognosis?

9. What happens next? Further surgery? Prosthesis? Rehabilitation?

10. Are there any clinical trials underway for new bone cancer treatments that I could be a part of?

GLOSSARY

antibiotic Substance that is able to kill bacteria.

biopsy Removal of a sample of tissue for laboratory tests.

bloodstream Flow of blood around the body.

bone graft Bone used to replace a missing portion of bone taken either from the person's body or from a donor.

cancellous Describing a type of spongy tissue inside bone.

cancer Disease caused by abnormal cells that destroy healthy tissue.

cartilage Strong, flexible type of connective tissue.

cell Basic unit of living things.

cell division Process by which a cell divides to form two new cells.

chemotherapy Chemical treatment for cancer.

chondrosarcoma Common form of bone cancer that arises in cartilage.

chordoma Type of bone cancer usually occurring in the spine.

computed tomography (CT) scan Scan using X-rays and radioactive dye.

DNA (deoxyribonucleic acid) Substance that carries the genetic information of an organism.

Ewing sarcoma Bone cancer that begins in immature nerve tissue within bone marrow.

immune system System in the body that recognizes and fights against disease.

magnetic resonance imaging (MRI) Noninvasive diagnostic procedure using a scanner to get detailed sectional images of the internal structure of the body.

metastasis Spread of a tumor from one part of the body to other parts.

mutation A change in genetic material.

neo-adjuvant chemotherapy Chemotherapy given prior to surgery to attempt to shrink the cancer so that the surgical procedure may not need to be as extensive.

oncology Study of cancerous tumors.

organ Part of the body that serves a specific function.

osteoblast Bone-forming cell.

osteochondroma The most common type of benign bone tumor.

osteoclast Bone cell that breaks down bone.

osteosarcoma Most common type of primary bone cancer.

primary bone cancer Cancer that begins in bone.

prostate Male gland that secretes fluid into semen (the fluid in sperm).

prosthesis Artificial device used to replace bone removed in surgery.

radioactive Emitting radiation.

subchondral Describing smooth bone tissue found in the joints.

tissue Group of cells in an organism.

tumor Abnormal mass of tissue.

virus Non-living particle that consists of genetic material inside a protein capsule.

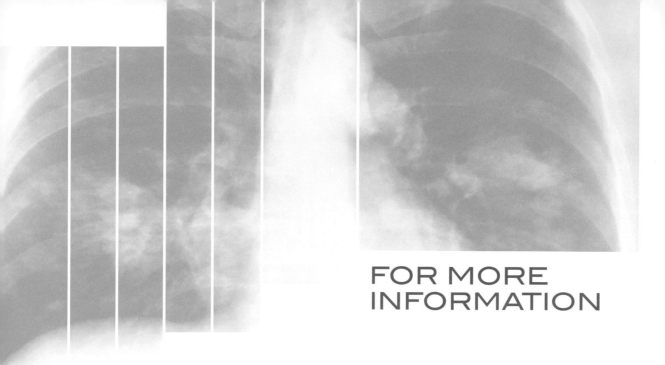

FOR MORE INFORMATION

American Academy of Orthopaedic Surgeons
6300 North River Road
Rosemont, IL 60018-4262
(800) 346-2267
Web site: http://orthoinfo.aaos.org
The AAOS provides information about the musculoskeletal system to
    surgeons and others throughout the world.

American Academy of Pediatrics
141 Northwest Point Boulevard
Elk Grove Village, IL 60007-1098
(847) 434-4000
Web site: http://www.aap.org
The American Academy of Pediatrics (AAP) is an organization
    made up of pediatricians committed to attaining the best
    physical, social, and mental health for infants, children, and
    adolescents.

American Cancer Society
1599 Clifton Road NE
Atlanta, GA 30329-4251
(800) 227-2345
Web site: http://www.cancer.org
The ACS is a nationwide, community-based health organization
   dedicated to cancer research and education, as well as patient
   services.

American Society of Clinical Oncology
1900 Duke Street, Suite 200
Alexandria, VA 22314
(703) 299-0150
Web site: http://www.asco.org
The ASCO is a non-profit organization with the goal of improving
   cancer care and prevention and ensuring that cancer patients
   receive quality care.

CureSearch National Childhood Cancer Foundation
4600 East West Highway, Suite 600
Bethesda, MD 20814-3457
(800) 458-6223
Web site: http://www.curesearch.org
CureSearch National Childhood Cancer Foundation supports childhood
   cancer research for the Children's Oncology Group (COG), the
   world's largest cooperative cancer research organization. This is a
   primary source for physicians for information about clinical trials
   and a variety of pediatric tumors, including bone tumors. The
   COG Web site (www.childrensoncologygroup.org) has good
   general information for non-physicians.

National Cancer Institute
6116 Executive Boulevard, Room 3036A
Bethesda, MD 20892
(800) 4-CANCER (422-6237)
Web site: http://www.cancer.gov
The National Cancer Institute is a component of National Institutes of
    Health. It is dedicated to the prevention, diagnosis, and treatment
    of cancer.

WEB SITES

Due to the changing nature of Internet links, Rosen Publishing has
developed an online list of Web sites related to the subject of this book.
This site is updated regularly. Please use this link to access the list:

http://www.rosenlinks.com/cms/bone

FOR FURTHER READING

Barr, Ronald, et al. *Childhood Cancer: Information for the Patient and Family*. Hamilton, ON, Canada: B. C. Decker, 2001.

Cristian, Adrian, M.D. *Lower Limb Amputation: A Guide to Living a Quality Life*. New York, NY: Demos Medical Publishing, 2005.

I Beat Cancer: 50 People Tell You How They Did It. Oxnard, CA: Awareness Publishing, 2003.

Meeks, Linda, and Philip Heit. *Health and Wellness*. New York, NY: McGraw-Hill/Glencoe, 2005.

Orr, Tamra. *Frequently Asked Questions About Bone Cancer* (FAQ: Teen Life). New York, NY: Rosen Publishing Group, Inc., 2008.

Panno, Joseph, Ph.D. *Cancer: The Roles of Genes, Lifestyle, and Environment*. New York, NY: Facts On File, 2004.

Royston, Angela. *Cancer*. Portsmouth, NH: Heinemann Library, 2006.

Silverstein, Alvin, et al. *Cancer: Conquering a Deadly Disease*. New York, NY: Twenty-First Century Books, 2004.

BIBLIOGRAPHY

American Cancer Society. "Cancer Reference Information" May 2006. Retrieved March 2008 (http://www.cancer.org/docroot/CRI/CRI_0.asp).

American Cancer Society. "Detailed Guide: Bone Cancer." 2008. Retrieved March 2008 (http://www.cancer.org/docroot/CRI/CRI_2_3x.asp?rnav=cridg&dt=2).

The Arthritis Society. "Paget's Disease." Reviewed December 21, 2007. Retrieved March 2008 (http://www.arthritis.ca/types%20of%20arthritis/pagets/default.asp).

Benowitz, Steven I. *Cancer*. Berkeley Heights, NJ: Enslow Publishers, 1999.

CancerBackup. "Primary Bone Cancer Information Centre." October 15, 2007. Retrieved March 2008 (http://www.cancerbackup.org.uk/Cancertype/Bone).

Cancer Information Network. "What Is Bone Cancer?: An Overview." TheCancer.info. December 2002. Retrieved March 2008 (http://www.cancerlinksusa.com/cancer/other/bone/index.asp).

Cancer Research UK. "Bone Cancer." February 2008. Retrieved March 2008 (http://www.cancerhelp.org.uk/help/default.asp?page=4404).

Eck, Jason C. "Bone Cancer." MedicineNet.com. August 2007. Retrieved March 2008 (http://www.medicinenet.com/bone_cancer/article.htm).

Eyre, Harmon. *Informed Decisions: Second Edition.* Atlanta, GA: American Cancer Society, 2002.

Genetics Home Reference. "Li-Fraumeni Syndrome." January 2007. Retrieved March 2008 (http://ghr.nlm.nih.gov/condition= lifraumenisyndrome).

Genetics Home Reference. "RECQL4." January 13, 2008. Retrieved March 2008 (http://ghr.nlm.nih.gov/gene=recql4).

Ingraham, J. L., and C. A. Ingraham. *Introduction to Microbiology.* 3rd ed. Pacific Grove, CA: Brooks/Cole-Thomson Learning, Inc., 2004.

Mayo Clinic. "Bone Cancer." Retrieved March 2008 (http://www.mayoclinic.com/health/bone-cancer/DS00520/DSECTION=1).

Mayo Clinic. "Erin Sweeney." Retrieved April 2008 (http://www.mayoclinic.org/patientstories/story-111.html).

MHE Research Foundation. "Multiple Hereditary Exostoses." Retrieved March 2008 (http://www.radix.net/~hogue/mhe.htm).

Miller, Robin E. "Types of Cancer Teens Get." *Kids Health.* June 2007. Retrieved March 2008 (http://www.kidshealth.org/teen/diseases_conditions/cancer/types_of_cancer.html).

Mr. Blogger. "Limbs of Steel." July 17, 2006. Retrieved March 2008 (http://prosthetics-and-orthotics.blogspot.com/2006_07_16_archive.html).

National Cancer Institute. "Bone Cancer." Retrieved March 2008 (http://www.cancer.gov/cancertopics/types/bone).

National Cancer Institute. "Bone Cancer: Questions and Answers." Retrieved March 2008 (http://www.cancer.gov/cancertopics/factsheet/Sites-Types/bone).

National Cancer Institute. "Experimental Drug for Osteosarcoma Improves Overall Survival." February 19, 2008. Retrieved March 2008 (http://www.cancer.gov/clinicaltrials/results/osteosarcoma0308).

Schilling, Ray. "Bone Cancer." Dr. Schilling's Net Health Book.
    November 2006. Retrieved March 2008 (http://www.nethealthbook.
    com/cancer_bonecancer.html).
Teen Info on Cancer. "Bone Cancer." June 2007. Retrieved March 2008
    (http://www.click4tic.org.uk/understandit/typesofcancer/bonecancer).
Thacker, Mihir, M.D. (reviewer). "Childhood Cancer: Osteosarcoma."
    Kids Health. January 2008. Retrieved March 2008 (http://kidshealth.
    org/parent/medical/cancer/cancer_osteosarcoma.html).
University of Virginia Health System. "Bone Disorders." August 21, 2006.
    Retrieved March 2008 (http://www.healthsystem.virginia.edu/uvahealth/
    adult_bone/chondrosar.cfm).

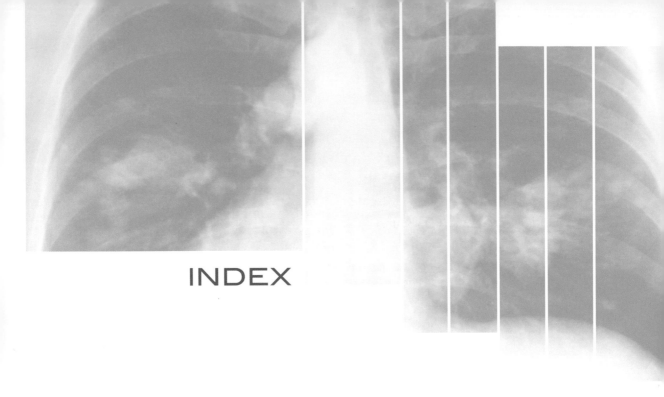

INDEX

ABOUT THE AUTHOR

Heather Hasan graduated from college summa cum laude with dual majors in chemistry and biochemistry. She has written many books about the chemical elements and has authored books on the subjects of astronomy and genetics. She also wrote *Cervical Cancer*, another title in Rosen's Cancer and Modern Science series. Hasan currently lives in Pennsylvania with her husband, Omar, and their sons, Samuel and Matthew.

PHOTO CREDITS

Cover, p.1 © SPL/Photo Researchers; cover corner photo, pp. 4–5 © Punchstock; pp. 4–5 (skeleton) www.istockphoto.com/John Woodcock; back cover and throughout, p. 18 © National Cancer Institute; pp. 5, 48 © AFP/Getty Images: p. 9 © www.istockphoto.com/ Mads Abildgaard; pp. 10, 29 © Schleichkorn/Custom Medical Stock Photo; pp. 12, 39 © Zephyr/Photo Researchers; p. 15 © CNRI/Photo Researchers; p. 16 © VEM/Photo Researchers; p. 21 © Parviz M. Pour/Photo Researchers; p. 25 © John Birdsall Photography/Custom Medical Stock Photo; p. 26 © www.istockphoto.com/Cliff Parnell; p. 31 © ISM/Phototake; p. 34 © www.istockphoto.com/Joseph Abbott; p. 37 © Collection CNRI/Phototake; p. 40 © Mauro Fermariello/Photo Researchers; p. 45 © AP Photos; p. 47 Courtesy of Ohio Wildwood.

Designer: Evelyn Horovicz; Editor: Christopher Roberts
Photo Researcher: Marty Levick